The New Investor's Guide

The New Investor's Guide, Volume 1

Kabir Kamboj

Published by Finletto by Sellbrochure, 2025.

THE NEW INVESTOR'S GUIDE

First edition. December 8, 2025.

ISBN: 979-8231683642

Written by Kabir Kamboj.

Table of Contents

BASICS OF STOCK MARKET FOR BEGINNERS

One of the most common reason why people are motivated to enter the stock market is due to the claims the sea on social media of others earning lakhs and crores of rupees unfortunately many individuals jump into the market without any proper analysis often investing in penny stocks which can lead to disasters losses the main goal of this book is to prevent such speculative gambles and help individuals avoid incurring avoidable losses

Through this book will take you on the journey of stock market starting from basics and progressing towards advanced stage of trading we will learn the fundamentals, various types of analysis , as well as different techniques,patterns, and strategies that I have acquired through my own experience.This book has been curated in such a way to provide all the vital knowledge in the simplest of language.Most people never receive proper financial education in school or college. As a result, they grow up knowing how to earn money but not how to manage or grow it. To become financially successful, every individual must take responsibility for learning how money works.

Mastering any subject requires time and consistent effort. Someone who studies a topic for an hour every day can become highly knowledgeable within a few years.

If a person increases their study time to several hours a day, this process becomes even faster. Many people assume that stock trading or investing is difficult, but in reality, simple methods can produce great results when they are practiced regularly and with discipline.

<u>Spending vs. Investing:</u>

If someone suddenly receives a large sum of money, their first thought is usually how to spend it. Only after the excitement fades does the idea of saving or investing appear. Keeping money in a bank savings account generally provides a very low return. Fixed deposits offer slightly higher interest, but still limited. Simply storing money is not enough because money loses value over time.

Understanding Inflation:

Inflation is a common economic process in which the general price level of goods and services increases over time. As prices rise, the value or purchasing power of money falls. The cost of commodities today is often significantly higher than it was a few years ago.

If money is stored without being invested, inflation gradually erodes its value. Therefore, making informed investment decisions is necessary to protect and grow wealth over time.

Identifying Suitable Investments:

Successful investing depends on the ability to separate sound investment opportunities from speculative or high-risk ones. Many people invest in assets such as real estate, insurance plans, mutual funds, or digital currencies without proper evaluation.

Sound investment decisions require research, planning, and an understanding of financial principles, rather than relying on guesswork or trends.

The Rule of 72:

The Rule of 72 is a simple method used to estimate the number of years required for an investment to double based on its annual rate of return. The formula is:

Years to Double = 72 ÷ Annual Rate of Return

For example: if an investor earns a 12% return annually, it will take approximately six years for their money to double (72 ÷ 12 = 6).

Investors often aim for opportunities where their capital can double in three to four years, provided the investment is reliable and sustainable.

CHAPTER 1 FUNDAMENTAL ANALYSIS

Fundamental analysis is a method used by investors to determine the true value of a company and its shares. Instead of focusing on short-term price movements, fundamental analysis examines the underlying factors that influence a company's performance over time. Its primary objective is to find stocks that are either undervalued or overvalued, and to make investment decisions based on this assessment.

At the core of fundamental analysis is the belief that the stock market may not always price a company accurately. Prices can fluctuate due to emotion, speculation, or temporary events. However, over the long run, stock prices tend to reflect the real strength and financial health of a business. Therefore, by studying a company's fundamentals, investors aim to identify profitable opportunities before the market fully recognizes them.

Fundamental analysis typically begins with a study of the company itself. Investors look at the business model, products or services offered, competitive position in the market, and quality of management. A business that has a sustainable competitive advantage, such as strong branding, patented technology, or efficient distribution, is usually considered a good long-term investment.

The next stage involves examining financial statements, which include the balance sheet, income statement, and cash flow statement. These documents help investors understand how much revenue the company generates, how much profit it earns, how efficiently it operates, and how well it manages its debt.

It is common to observe stock prices increase beyond the intrinsic value . In such a situation the question arises as to whether one should buy the stock or not. To answer this question, it initial to understand the concept of how price tends to Exceed intrinsic value. Ratios play a significant role in investing , for example: **PE ratio,PB ratio ,debt ratio** and **current ratio** are portrayed as complicated and challenging to understand, leading many to believe that they are only for finance professionals. My goal is to explain these terms in the simplest way possible just as I came to understand them.

(PRICE/EARNING RATIO)PE RATIO

The **Price-to-Earnings (P/E)** ratio is one of the most widely used valuation tools in the stock market. It helps investors understand whether a stock is priced fairly in relation to the company's earnings.

The **P/E ratio** is calculated by dividing the current market price of a share by the **earnings per share (EPS)** of the company:

P/E Ratio = Market Price per Share ÷ Earnings per Share (EPS)

This ratio shows how much an investor is willing to pay for every one rupee of earnings generated by the company. For example, if a company has a P/E ratio of 20, it means investors are willing to pay ₹20 for every ₹1 of earnings.

A **high P/E** ratio generally indicates that the market expects strong future growth from the company. Investors believe the company's profits will rise in the coming years, so they are ready to pay a premium today. High P/E stocks are often found in fast-growing sectors like technology, consumer brands, or pharmaceutical companies.

A **lower P/E** ratio often indicates potential benefits for investors, but it must be understood in the proper context. When a stock has a low P/ E, it generally means the market price is low relative to the company's earnings. In simple terms, you are paying less money for every rupee of profit the company makes. For value investors, this can be attractive because there is a possibility that the stock is **undervalued** and may rise in price when the market recognizes its true worth.

However, a low P/E ratio is beneficial **only when the company has strong fundamentals** such as consistent profits, low debt, good management, and steady growth prospects. In such cases, a low P/E can present a good opportunity to buy a quality company at a reasonable price.

On the other hand, investors should be cautious because a low P/E does **not always guarantee a good investment.** Sometimes, a stock may have a low P/E because the business is facing problems such as declining sales, poor management decisions, legal challenges, or a slowdown in the industry.

A lower P/E ratio often suggests better value, but only if the company's fundamentals support future growth.

(DEBT/EQUITY RATIO)DEBT RATIO

The **debt ratio** is a financial metric that measures how much of a company's assets are financed through debt. It shows the proportion of total assets that have been funded by borrowing rather than by the company's own equity.

Debt Ratio = Total Debt ÷ Total Assets

A **high debt ratio** indicates that a large portion of the company's assets are financed by loans or borrowings. This may increase financial risk, because the company must regularly pay interest and repay principal, even if business conditions become difficult.

A **low debt ratio** means that the company relies less on borrowing. Such companies are generally considered financially stable, because they have fewer fixed obligations and more flexibility to manage their operations.

Suppose a company has the following financial information:

Total Assets: ₹50,00,000

Total Debt: ₹20,00,000

Debt Ratio = 20,00,000 ÷ 50,00,000 = **0.40**

This means the company has a debt ratio of **0.40**, or **40%.**

A **40%** debt ratio indicates that 40% of the company's assets are financed using borrowed money.

The remaining **60%** of assets are financed through equity or internal funds.A ratio of 0.40 is generally considered moderate.The company has some debt, but it is not excessively dependent on borrowing.

This level of debt may be manageable as long as the company has consistent earnings to pay interest and principal.

CURRENT RATIO(CURRENT ASSETS/CURRENT LIABILITIES)

The current ratio is a liquidity measurement that shows a company's ability to pay its short-term obligations using its short-term assets. It tells investors whether a business has enough resources to cover its bills, expenses, and debts that are due within one year.

Current Ratio = Current Assets ÷ Current Liabilities

Current Assets: cash, inventory, receivables, and other assets that can be converted into cash within 12 months

Current Liabilities: short-term debts, payable amounts, and obligations due within 12 months

Suppose a company has the following financial information:

Current Assets: ₹8,00,000

Current Liabilities: ₹4,00,000

Current Ratio = 8,00,000 ÷ 4,00,000 = 2.0

A current ratio of 2.0 means the company has **₹2 in current assets for every ₹1 in current liabilities.**

This indicates strong liquidity and the ability to meet short-term financial obligations comfortably.

What Is a Good Current Ratio?

Current Ratio > 1: Generally considered safe (assets are more than liabilities).

Current Ratio = 1: Borderline situation (assets equal liabilities).

Current Ratio < 1: Risky (company may struggle to pay short-term debts).

BOOK VALUE PER SHARE

Book Value Per Share (BVPS) tells investors how much each share of a company would be worth if the company sold all its assets and paid off all its liabilities. It represents the actual value of a company's net assets for each outstanding share.

Book Value Per Share = (Total Assets – Total Liabilities) ÷ Number of Outstanding Shares

A higher book value per share suggests that the company has strong underlying asset value. If a stock's market price is close to or lower than its book value per share, it may indicate that the stock is undervalued.

Suppose a company has:

Total Assets: ₹50,00,000

Total Liabilities: ₹20,00,000

Shareholders' Equity = Total Assets – Total Liabilities

= ₹50,00,000 – ₹20,00,000

= ₹30,00,000

Step 2: Find the number of outstanding shares

Assume the company has 3,00,000 shares outstanding.

Step 3: Apply the BVPS formula

Book Value Per Share = Shareholders' Equity ÷ Number of Shares

= ₹30,00,000 ÷ 3,00,000

= ₹10 per share

Price-to-Sales (P/S) Ratio

The Price-to-Sales Ratio is a financial metric used to evaluate how much investors are paying for every rupee of a company's sales. It compares a company's **market value** to its **total revenue**, helping investors understand whether a stock is expensive or cheap relative to the revenue it generates. This ratio is especially useful for analyzing companies that do not have stable profits yet, such as start-ups or high-growth businesses.

Price to sales ratio=(Market price per share/sale per share)

A **lower P/S** ratio generally indicates the stock may be undervalued, meaning investors are paying less for each rupee of sales.

A **higher P/S** ratio suggests the stock may be overvalued, meaning investors are paying more for each rupee of sales.

A company has:

Market price: ₹200 per share

Sales per share: ₹100

P/S Ratio=200/100=**2**

This means investors are paying ₹2 for every ₹1 of sales generated by the company.

CHAPTER 2 TECHNICAL ANALYSIS

Technical analysis is a method of evaluating stocks by studying market data such as **price movement, trading volume, and chart patterns.** Instead of focusing on company fundamentals like revenue, profit, or balance sheet, technical analysis examines how a stock's price behaves in the market. It is based on the belief that all relevant information is already reflected in the stock price and that prices move in trends which can be identified and used to predict future movements.

Technical analysts use **stock charts** to observe historical price changes and spot patterns that often repeat over time. I have encountered many individuals who received a simple challenge to be difficult and ended up making it so. Many people perceive a paper or screen full of graphs and numbers to be complex and difficult. When they hear the term technical their mind immediately assumes it to be complex and challenging. To dispel this notion I will explain technical analysis in the simplest way possible

So let's delve into what it actually means. Technical analysis involves studying charts and price action to determine the likelihood of price increases or decreases. Therefore technical analysis helps determine the best time to buy or sell a stock and how long one should hold on to it

The term trends is commonly used to describe things that are currently popular or becoming so. In the field of stock market the investor and traders must be aware of certain types of trends. A trend refers to the fluctuation in the stock price. Identify these trend is crucial, the price action be offence see is never a straight line, it has zigzag fluctuation but always head in a certain direction

The three type of trends based on the direction of the graph:

- A **downward trend** is observed when the fluctuations are going downward. When the price keeps making lower highs and lower lows, it shows sellers are dominating and the stock price is generally falling

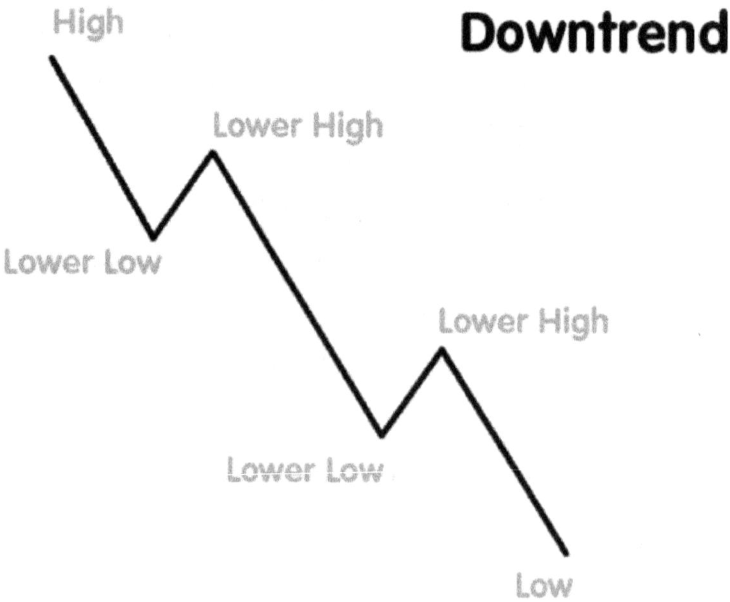

A downtrend is a market condition where a stock's price keeps moving lower over time. It is identified by a series of lower highs and lower lows, showing that sellers are stronger than buyers. In a downtrend, supply is higher than demand, causing prices to fall. Traders usually avoid buying in a downtrend because it signals negative momentum and declining stock value.

- An **upward trend** is observed when the fluctuations are going down. When the price keeps making higher highs and higher lows, it indicates that buyers are in control and the stock price is generally rising.

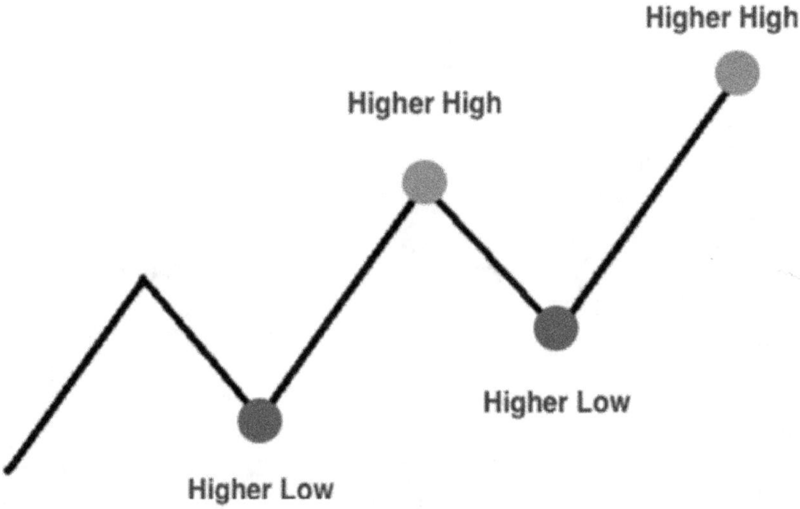

An uptrend is a market condition where a stock's price keeps moving higher over time. It is identified by a series of higher highs and higher lows, showing that buyers are stronger than sellers. In an uptrend, demand increases, pushing prices upward. Traders usually look to buy during an uptrend because it signals positive momentum and growth in stock value.

- **Sideways (range bound)**When the price moves within a fixed range without clear upward or downward movement, it signals that neither buyers nor sellers have strong control.

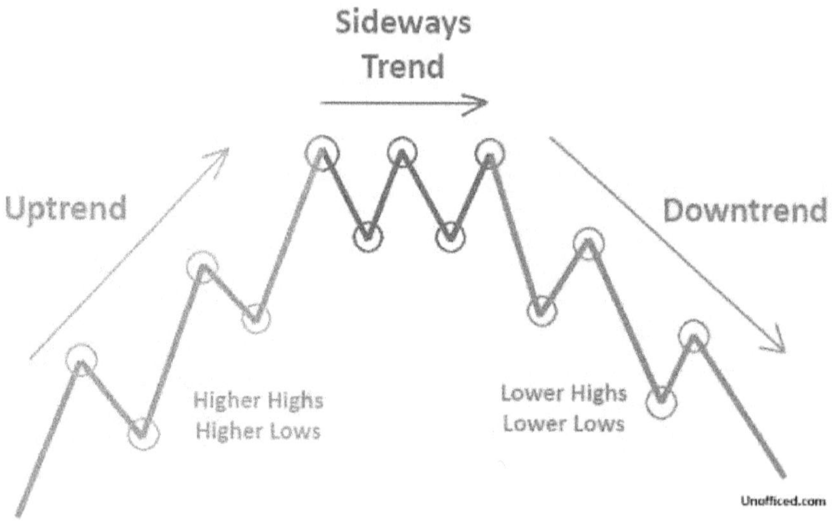

A SIDEWAYS TREND OCCURS when a stock's price moves within a fixed range without rising or falling significantly. It shows that neither buyers nor sellers are in control. Prices typically move between a support level (bottom) and a resistance level (top). During a sideways trend, traders often wait for a breakout before making major buy or sell decisions.

CHAPTER 3 SUPPORT AND RESISTANCE

S**UPPORT:** Support is a price level where a stock tends to stop falling and start rising. It works like a "floor" in the market. When the price reaches support, buyers usually enter, creating demand and pushing the price up. If support is broken, it may indicate further downside movement. Support helps traders identify potential buying opportunities.

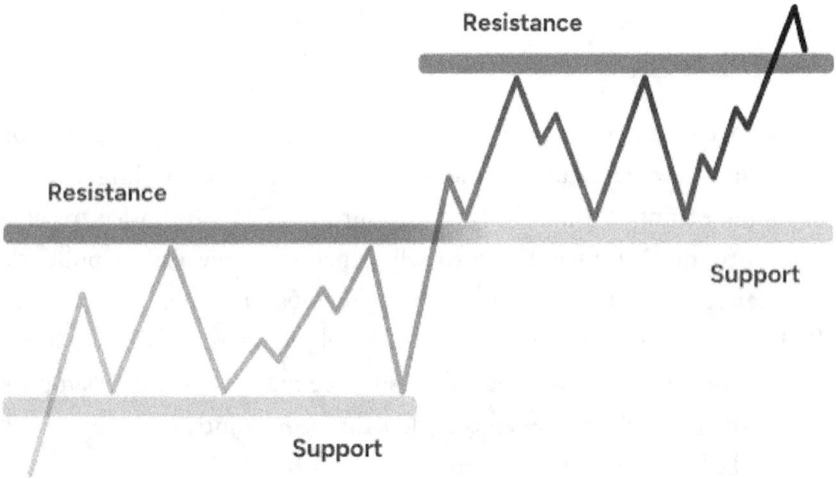

Support is a key concept in technical analysis that refers to a price level where a stock tends to stop falling and may start rising again. It acts like a floor where buying interest becomes strong enough to overcome selling pressure. When the price approaches support, traders expect a bounce upward because buyers step in at this level. Support is identified by looking at previous price lows on a chart. If the price breaks below support, it may continue to fall to a new lower level. Understanding support helps traders find potential entry points and manage risk in the stock market.

RESISTANCE:

Resistance is a price level in technical analysis where a stock tends to stop rising and may start falling. It acts like a ceiling, where selling pressure becomes stronger than buying pressure. When the price reaches resistance, many traders begin to sell, expecting a reversal or pullback. Resistance is identified by looking at previous price highs on a chart. If the stock breaks above a resistance level with strong volume, it can create a new uptrend and that old resistance may become new support. Understanding resistance helps traders find exit points, set target prices, and make better market decisions.

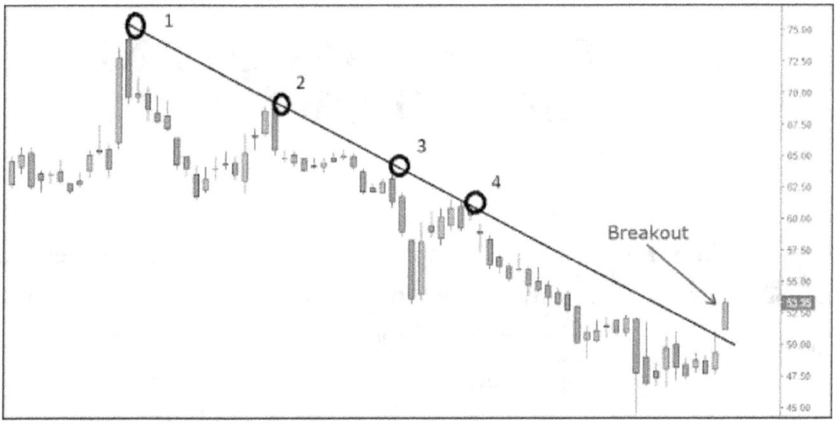

Traders identify resistance by studying past price charts and marking points where rallies have repeatedly failed. When the price approaches resistance, traders expect potential reversals, pullbacks, or consolidation. However, if the stock breaks above resistance with strong trading volume, it signals buying strength and may lead to a new uptrend. In such cases, the old resistance often becomes new support.

CHAPTER 4 BREAKOUT AND BREAKDOWN

A **breakout** occurs when a stock's price moves above a defined resistance level with strong volume. It signals that buyers have gained control and the price may continue rising. **Breakouts** often indicate the beginning of a new uptrend. Traders look for breakouts to enter buy positions, expecting higher prices. A valid breakout usually requires high trading volume to confirm strength.

After a breakout, prices often continue to rise because previous sellers are no longer able to hold the price down. In many cases, the old resistance level becomes a new support. Traders look for breakouts to enter long positions and capture upward momentum. Breakouts commonly occur from chart patterns such as triangles, flags, rectangles, and ranges.

On the other hand,a **breakdown** happens when the price of a stock falls below a key support level, where buyers previously stepped in to stop price declines. When support is broken, it signals strong selling pressure, meaning traders expect further price drops. Similar to breakouts, a

breakdown is more trustworthy when it occurs with **high volume**, confirming that sellers are active.

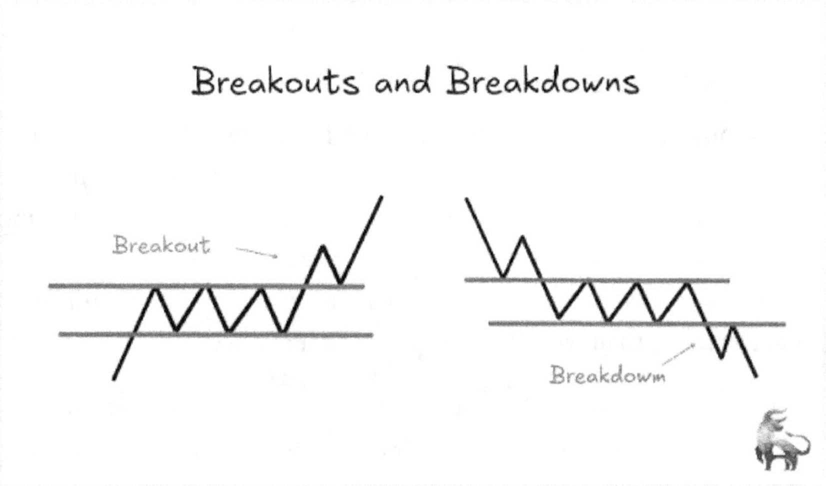

After a **breakdown**, prices often continue to fall because previous buyers can no longer keep the price stable. The old support level may become a new resistance. Traders use breakdowns to enter short positions or exit their holdings to avoid losses. Breakdowns often occur from patterns such as descending triangles, head and shoulders, and sideways ranges.

Breakout = Price moves above resistance , Uptrend likely

Breakdown = Price moves below support , Downtrend likely

CHAPTER 5 CANDLESTICK CHART PATTERNS

Candlestick patterns are a type of price chart used in technical analysis to show how a stock's price moves during a specific time period. Each "candlestick" represents four key prices: the opening, closing, highest, and lowest price of that period. The body of the candle shows the difference between the open and close, while the thin lines, called wicks or shadows, show the high and low prices.

Candlestick patterns help traders understand **market sentiment** — whether buyers (bulls) or sellers (bears) are in control. By studying patterns, traders try to predict **future price movements**.

There are two main types of candlesticks:

Bullish candles: Closing price is higher than opening price (shows buying pressure).

Bearish candles: Closing price is lower than opening price (shows selling pressure).

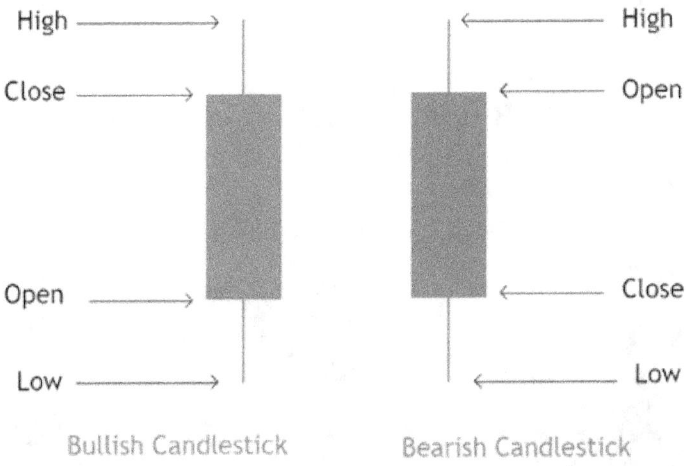

Candlestick patterns can be single candle patterns (like **Doji, Hammer, or Shooting Star**) or multiple candle patterns (like **Engulfing, Morning Star, and Head & Shoulders**).

Traders use candlestick patterns to identify **trend reversals, breakouts, and market entry or exit points,** making them a powerful tool in technical analysis.

TYPES OF CANDLES:

1.GREEN OR BULLISH CANDLE:

A green or bullish candle represents a period in which a stock's closing price is higher than its opening price. This indicates that buyers were in control during that time and pushed the price upward. The candle body shows the difference between the open and close, while the upper and lower wicks show the highest and lowest prices reached. A long bullish candle usually signals strong buying momentum, while a small bullish candle may show limited upward movement. Green or bullish candles are used by traders to identify uptrends, breakouts, and buying pressure in the market.

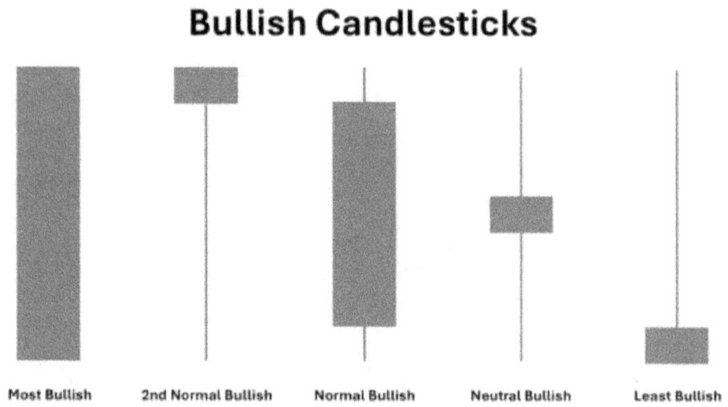

A bullish candle forms when the closing price is higher than the opening price, showing buying pressure. It usually indicates upward momentum.

2.RED OR BEARISH CANDLE

A red or bearish candle represents a period in which a stock's closing price is lower than its opening price. This indicates that sellers were in control and pushed the price downward. The body of the candle shows the difference between the open and close, while the upper and lower wicks show the highest and lowest prices reached during that time. A long bearish candle usually signals strong selling pressure, while a small bearish candle shows limited downward movement. Red or bearish candles help traders identify downtrends, breakdowns, and selling strength in the market.

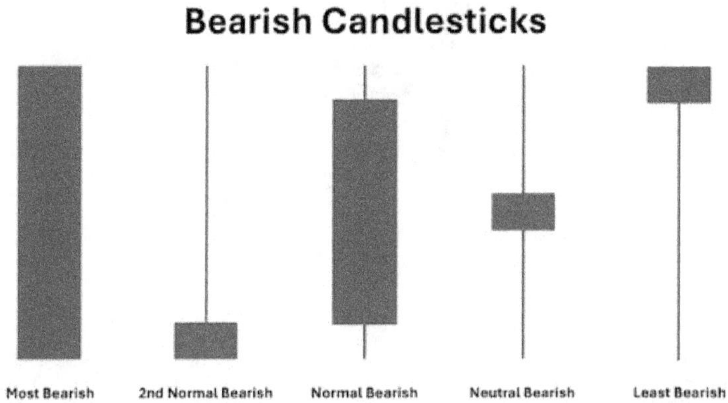

A bearish candle forms when the closing price is lower than the opening price, showing selling pressure. It usually indicates downward momentum

SINGLE CANDLESTICK PATTERNS

1. HAMMER AND HANGING MAN

A **Hammer** is a bullish reversal candlestick pattern that usually appears after a downtrend. It has a small body near the top of the candle and a long lower wick, showing that sellers pushed the price down during the period but buyers later took control and drove the price back up. This shift from selling to buying pressure signals that the downtrend may be coming to an end. A Hammer suggests a possible trend reversal to the upside, especially when confirmed by higher volume and a bullish candle afterward.

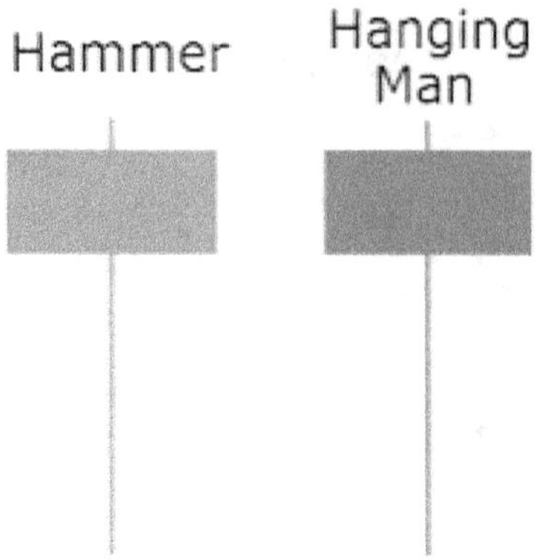

Hammer = Bullish signal (after downtrend).

A **Hanging Man** looks similar to a Hammer but appears after an uptrend, making it a bearish reversal pattern. It has a small body near the top and a long lower wick, showing that sellers tried to push prices down during the period. Even though the price recovered, the presence of selling pressure indicates weakness in the uptrend. A Hanging Man warns that the current upward movement may be slowing and a downward reversal could follow, especially if confirmed with a bearish candle or high trading volume.

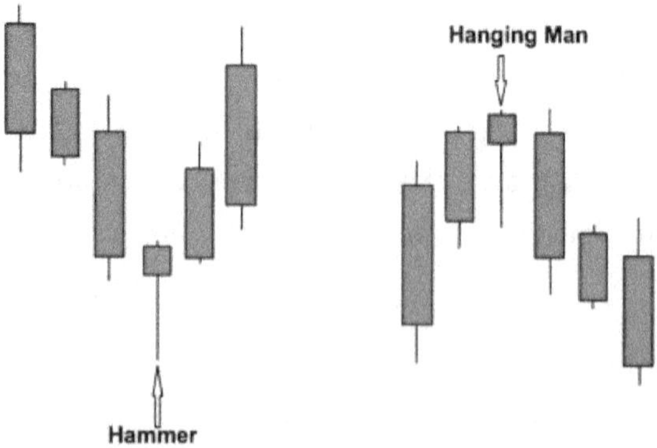

Hanging Man = Bearish signal (after uptrend).

1. INVERTED HAMMER AND SHOOTING STAR

An **Inverted Hammer** is a bullish reversal candlestick pattern that appears after a downtrend. It has a small body near the bottom of the candle and a long upper wick. The long wick shows that buyers tried to push the price higher, but sellers pulled it back down before closing. Even though the close is lower than the high, the presence of buying pressure signals a possible shift in momentum. The Inverted Hammer suggests that the downtrend may be weakening and a trend reversal to the upside could follow, especially if confirmed by a strong bullish candle afterward.

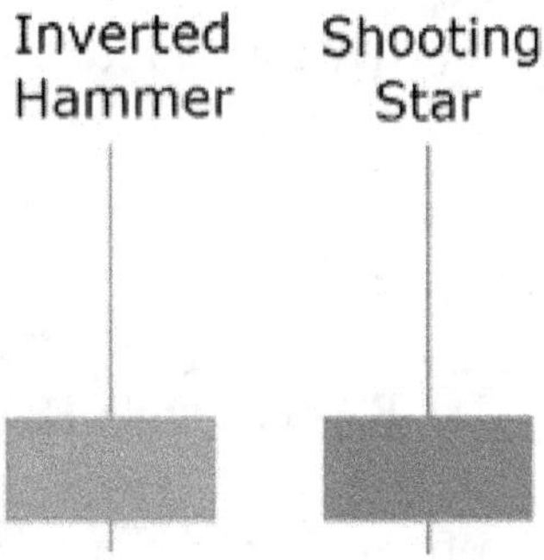

Inverted Hammer =Bullish signal (after downtrend).

A **Shooting Star** is a bearish reversal candlestick pattern that appears after an uptrend. It has a small body near the bottom of the candle and a long upper wick, which shows that buyers tried to push prices higher but failed to hold those levels. Sellers then took control, forcing the price back down. This indicates weakness in the uptrend. A Shooting Star warns that the price may reverse downward, especially if confirmed by a bearish candle or high volume.

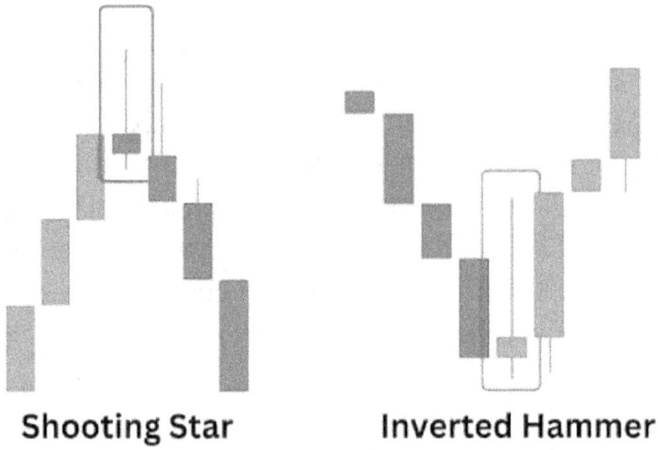

Shooting Star =Bearish signal (after uptrend).

1. DRAGONFLY DOJI AND GRAVESTONE DOJI

A **Dragonfly Doji** is a candlestick pattern where the opening, closing, and high prices are almost the same, with a long lower wick and little to no upper wick. It usually appears after a downtrend and shows that sellers pushed the price down significantly during the session, but buyers later stepped in and brought it back to the opening level. This change in sentiment signals buying strength and a possible bullish reversal. The Dragonfly Doji is more reliable when confirmed by a strong bullish candle on the next trading session.

DRAGONFLY DOJI

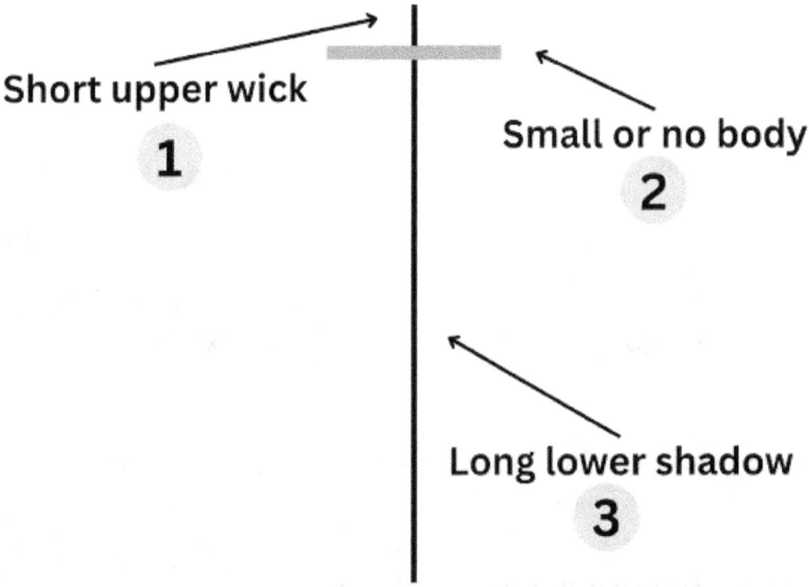

Dragonfly Doji = Bullish signal (long lower wick, after downtrend).

A **Gravestone Doji** is a candlestick pattern where the opening, closing, and low prices are almost the same, with a long upper wick and little to no lower wick. It usually appears after an uptrend and shows that buyers pushed the price up during the session, but sellers later took control and brought it back to the opening level. This shift indicates selling pressure and a possible bearish reversal. A Gravestone Doji becomes more meaningful when followed by a bearish candle or high selling volume.

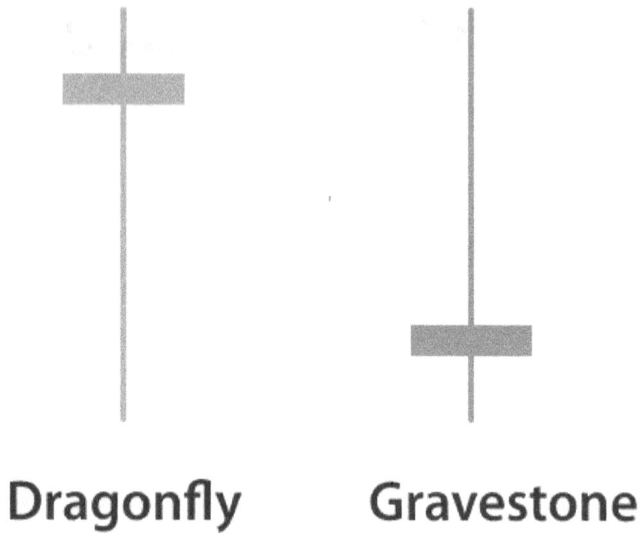

Gravestone Doji = Bearish signal (long upper wick, after uptrend).

DOUBLE CANDLESTICK PATTERNS

1. BULLISH AND BEARISH HARAMI

A **Bullish Harami** is a **two-candle reversal** pattern that appears **after a downtrend**. The first candle is a large bearish candle, showing strong selling pressure. The second candle is a **small bullish** candle that is fully contained within the body of the previous candle. This pattern signals that selling momentum is weakening and buyers may be gaining control. The small second candle represents indecision or a pause in the downtrend. A bullish Harami suggests a possible upward reversal, especially when confirmed by a bullish candle on the next trading day or an increase in trading volume.

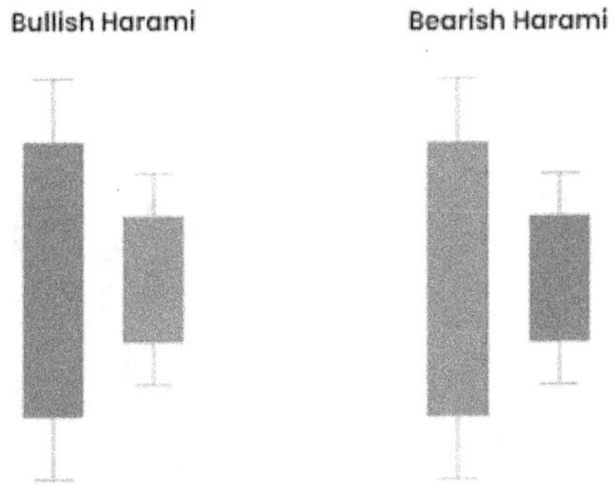

Bullish Harami =Appears after a downtrend, signals upward reversal.

A **Bearish Harami** is a **two-candle reversal pattern** that appears **after an uptrend.** The first candle is a large bullish candle, showing strong buying pressure. The second candle is a **small bearish** or **neutral candle** that stays completely inside the body of the previous candle. This pattern indicates that buying momentum is slowing down and sellers may be entering the market. The second small candle shows indecision after a strong rally, warning of a potential downward reversal. A bearish Harami becomes more reliable when followed by a bearish candle or a drop in trading volume.

Bearish Harami

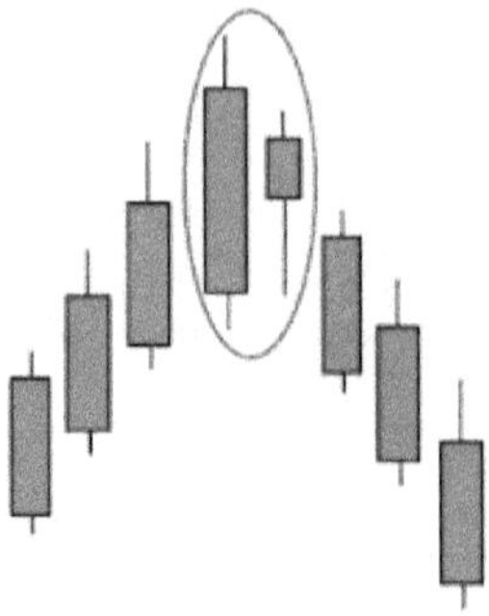

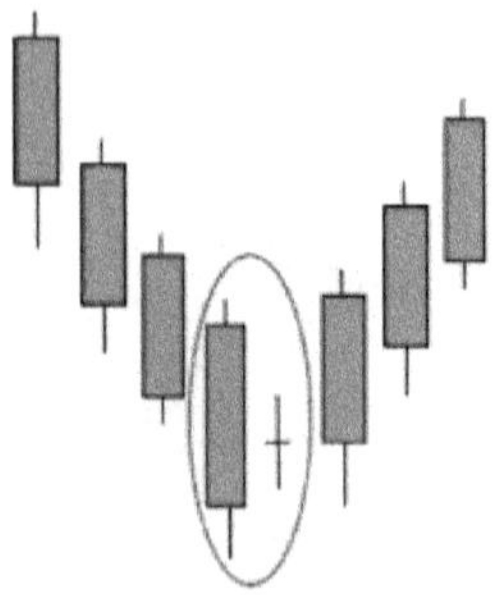

Bullish Harami Cross

Bearish Harami = Appears after an uptrend, signals downward reversal.

1. BULLISH ENGULFING AND BEARISH ENGULFING PATTERNS

A **Bullish Engulfing** is a **two-candle reversal pattern** that appears after a **downtrend**. The first candle is a **small bearish candle**, showing continued selling pressure. The second candle is a large bullish candle that completely **engulfs the body** of the previous candle. This means the second candle opens lower and closes higher than the first candle's range. A bullish engulfing pattern shows a strong shift from sellers to buyers, signaling that an uptrend may begin. The larger the second candle, the stronger the buying momentum. Traders often look for volume confirmation to increase reliability.

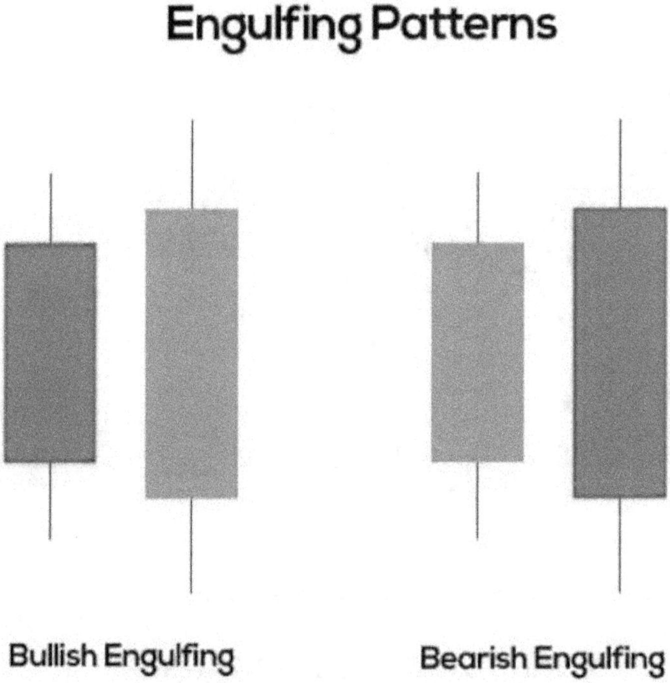

Bullish Engulfing = Downtrend to uptrend signal (buyers take control).

A **Bearish Engulfing** is a **two-candle reversal** pattern that appears after an uptrend. The first candle is a small bullish candle, showing continued buying pressure. The second candle is a large bearish candle that completely **engulfs** the body of the previous candle. This means the second candle opens higher and closes lower than the first candle's range. A bearish engulfing pattern shows a clear shift from buyers to sellers, signaling a **possible downward reversal**. The stronger and longer the second bearish candle, the greater the selling pressure and the higher the chance of a trend change.

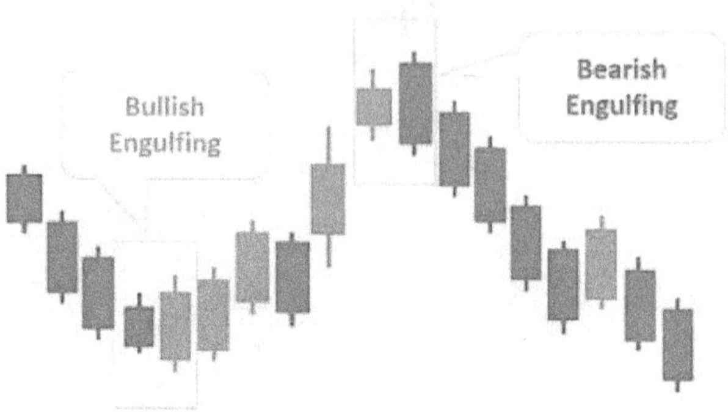

Bearish Engulfing = Uptrend to downtrend signal (sellers take control).

THREE CANDLESTICK PATTERNS

1. MORNING STAR AND EVENING STAR

A **Morning Star** is a **three-candle bullish reversal pattern** that appears after a downtrend.

The **first candle** is a long bearish candle, showing strong selling pressure.

The **second candle** is a small candle (bullish, bearish, or a Doji) that shows indecision and a slowdown in the downtrend.

The **third candle** is a strong bullish candle that closes well into the body of the first candle, proving that buyers have taken control.

The **Morning Star** signals that selling has weakened and buying may increase, indicating a potential trend reversal to the upside, especially when confirmed by high trading volume or a break above resistance.

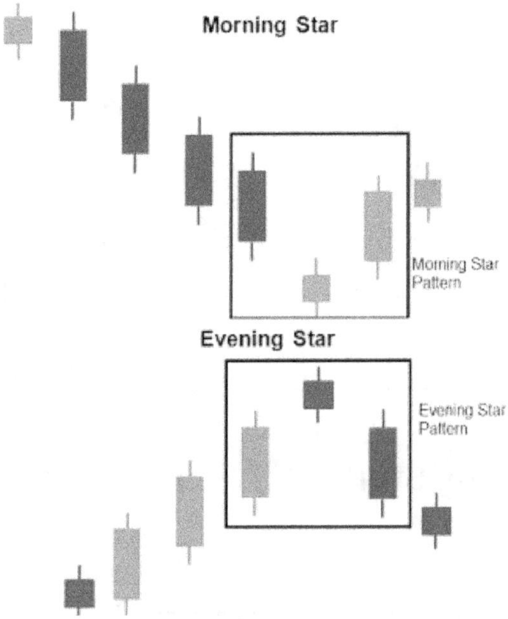

Morning Star =Bullish reversal (after a downtrend).

AN **Evening Star** is a **three-candle bearish reversal** pattern that appears after an uptrend.

The **first candle** is a long bullish candle, showing strong buying pressure.

The **second candle** is a small candle (bullish, bearish, or a Doji) that shows indecision and slowing momentum in the uptrend.

The **third candle** is a strong bearish candle that closes well into the body of the first candle, proving that sellers have taken control.

The **Evening Star** warns that buyers are losing strength and a downtrend may begin, especially when confirmed by high trading volume or a break below support

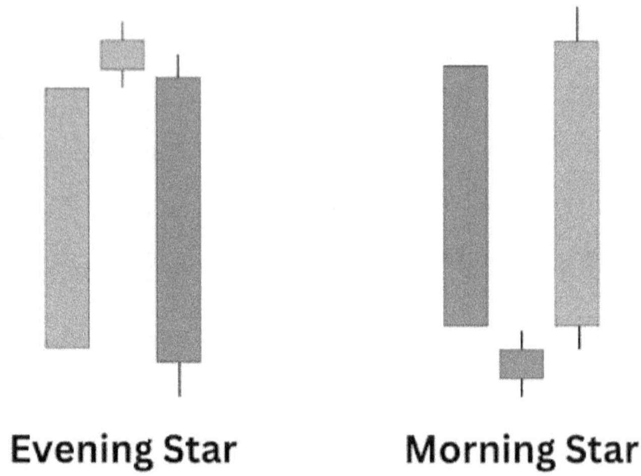

Evening Star = Bearish reversal (after an uptrend).

1. **BULLISH ABANDONED BABY AND BEARISH ABANDONED BABY**

A **Bullish Abandoned Baby** is a rare and strong bullish reversal pattern that appears after a downtrend.

It is a **three-candle pattern**.

Structure:

1. **First candle**: Long bearish candle (strong selling pressure).

2. **Second candle**: A Doji that gaps down from the first candle, meaning:

There is no overlap between the first candle's body and the Doji.Shows extreme indecision.

3. **Third candle**: Long bullish candle that gaps up from the Doji and closes well into the first candle's body.

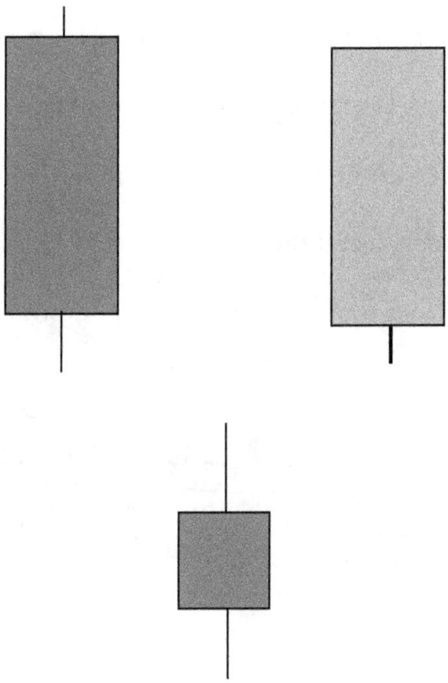

Bears (sellers) are fully in control initially.

The gap-down Doji shows exhaustion of sellers and indecision.

The gap-up bullish candle signals **buyers have taken over strongly.**

A likely trend reversal upward (buy signal).

A **Bearish Abandoned Baby** is a strong bearish reversal pattern that appears after an uptrend.

It is also a three-candle pattern but opposite.

Structure:

1. **First candle**: Long bullish candle (strong buying pressure).

2. **Second candle**: A Doji that gaps up from the first candle, meaning:

No overlap between the first candle's body and the Doji.

Shows extreme indecision at the top.

3. **Third candle**: Long bearish candle that gaps down from the Doji and closes well into the first candle's body.

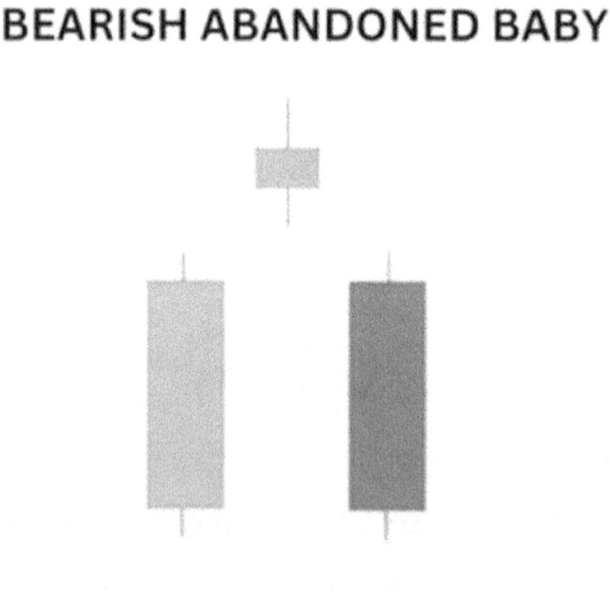

BULLS (BUYERS) are initially dominating.

The **gap-up** Doji shows buyers are losing strength and the trend is pausing.

The **gap-down** bearish candle indicates sellers have taken control.

A likely trend reversal downward (**sell signal**).

1. **THREE WHITE SOLDIER AND THREE BLACK CROWS**

The **Three White Soldiers pattern** is a powerful **bullish candlestick reversal** that usually appears after a significant downtrend or a long period of consolidation. The pattern consists of **three** consecutive **long green candles**, each opening within the body of the previous candle and closing progressively higher. This formation shows that **buyers** are consistently entering the market and pushing prices **upward** throughout three trading sessions.

For this pattern to be reliable, the candles should not have very long upper wicks, as that can indicate hesitation. Ideally, each candle closes near its high, showing strong momentum. Confirmation from higher trading volume makes this pattern more valid. After this pattern appears, traders often expect a **sustained uptrend**, as market sentiment has shifted from bearish to bullish convincingly.

Three consecutive long bullish (green) candles

Each candle opens within the body of the **previous** candle

Each candle closes **higher** than the previous candle

THE **Three Black Crows pattern** is a strong **bearish** candlestick reversal that generally forms after an uptrend or near major resistance levels. It consists of three long red candles, each opening within the body of the previous candle and closing lower every session. This sequence shows consistent selling pressure, with bears gradually taking control of the market.

To increase its reliability, the candles should close near their lows and should not have long lower wicks. Long wicks indicate uncertainty or buyer attempts to push prices up. High selling volume makes the signal stronger. After this pattern forms, many traders **expect a downtrend** or **continued bearish** movement, as market confidence shifts from optimism to caution or fear.

Three Black Crows

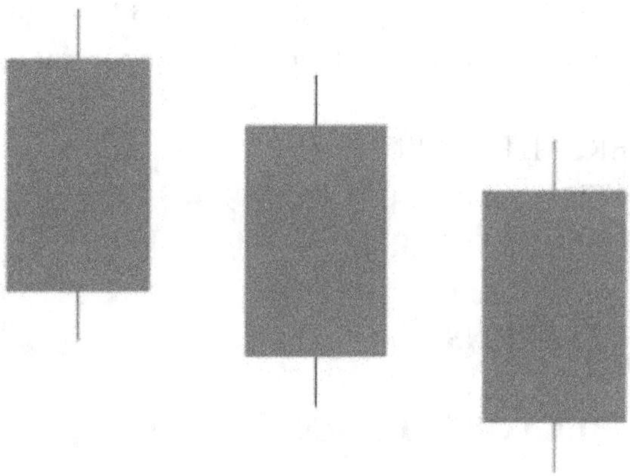

Three consecutive long bearish (**red**) candles

Each candle opens **within** the body of the previous candle

Each candle **closes lower** than the previous candle

CHAPTER 6 CHART PATTERNS

My sole intention is to provide you with quality information in one place and through one medium,this chapter focuses on chart patterns . The stock market charts reflect patterns that can be analysed under three categories. These charts show three important patterns.

1. REVERSAL PATTERNS
2. CONTINUATION PATTERNS
3. NEUTRAL PATTERNS

REVERSAL PATTERNS

1. DOUBLE TOP PATTERN

A **Double Top** is a common **bearish reversal** chart **pattern** that signals the end of an uptrend and the possible start of a downtrend. It forms when the price rises to a certain level, pulls back, and then rises again to the same level but fails to break above it. This creates **two peaks (tops)** at roughly the same price.

Between the two tops, the price declines to a support level known as the neckline. The pattern is considered complete when the price breaks below the neckline after forming the second top. This breakdown confirms that buyers are losing strength and sellers are taking control.

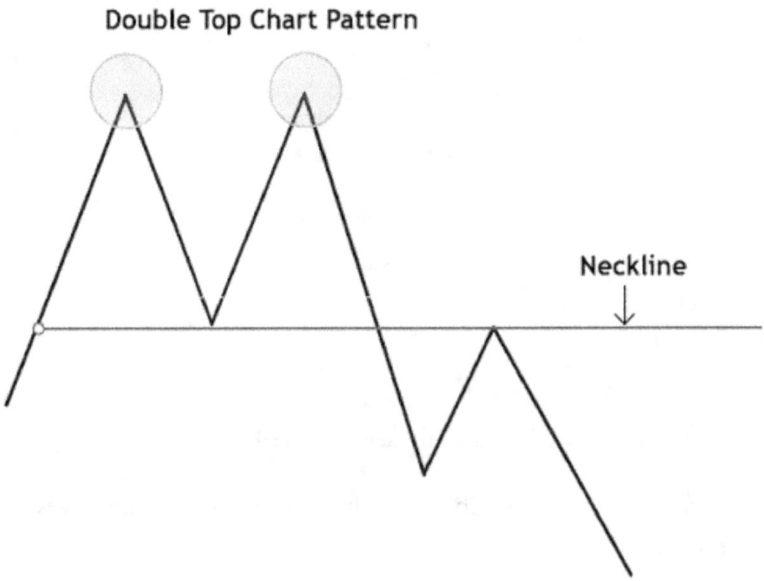

Market Psychology:

First Top: Buyers push price up but meet resistance.

Pullback: Sellers push price down to support.

Second Top: Buyers try again but fail near the same level.

Breakdown: Sellers gain momentum and start a new downtrend.

The pattern is **bearish**, usually used as a **sell signal**.

A **breakdown** below the neckline on high volume gives stronger confirmation.

Traders often set a target price by measuring the height from the tops to the neckline and projecting it downward.

1. **DOUBLE BOTTOM PATTERN**

A **Double Bottom** is a classic **bullish reversal chart pattern** that signals the end of a downtrend and the potential start of an uptrend. It forms when the price falls to a certain support level, bounces up, and then drops again to the same support level but fails to break below it. This creates **two lows** (**bottoms**) at roughly the same price.

Between the two bottoms, the price rises to a resistance level known as the **neckline**. The pattern is confirmed when the price **breaks above the neckline** after forming the second bottom. This breakout indicates that sellers are losing strength and buyers are taking control.

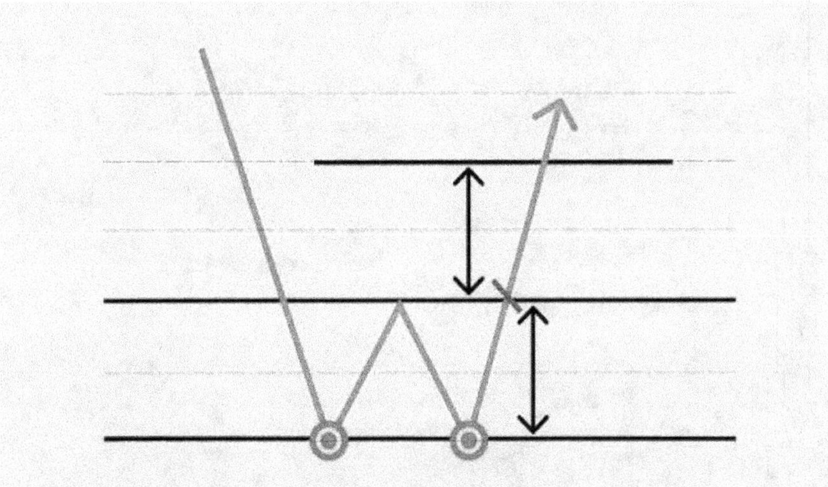

Market Psychology:

First Bottom: Sellers push price down but support holds.

Bounce: Buyers step in and lift the price.

Second Bottom: Sellers try again but fail at the same support level.

Breakout: Buyers gain momentum and start a new uptrend.

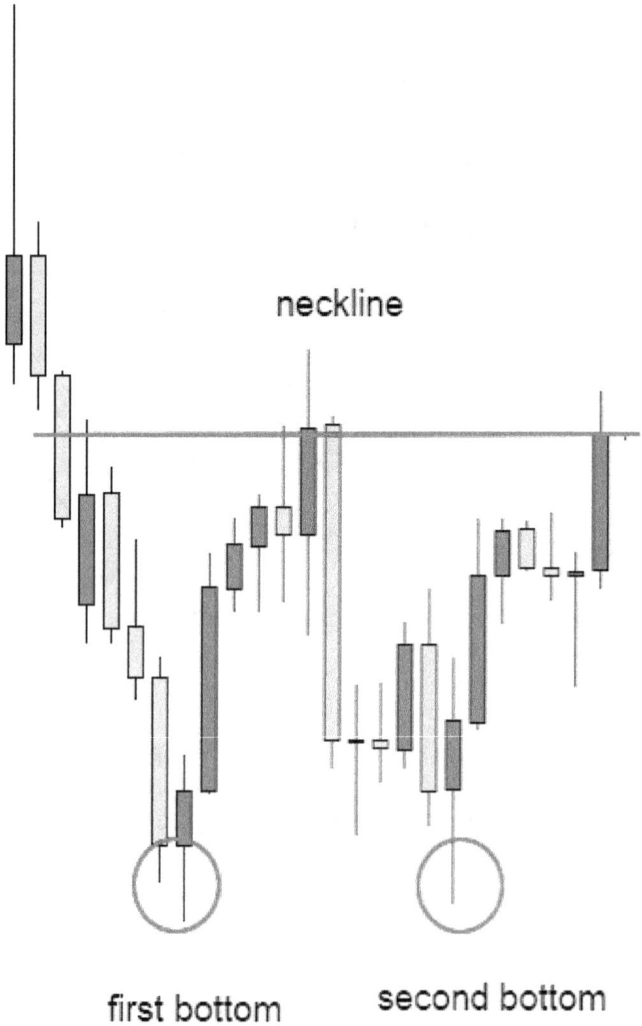

The **pattern** is **bullish** and used for **buy entries**.

A **breakout** above the **neckline** on **high volume** gives stronger confirmation.

Traders measure the height between the bottoms and neckline to estimate the **upside target**.

1. HEAD AND SHOULDER PATTERN

The **Head and Shoulders pattern** is one of the most reliable **bearish reversal** chart patterns in technical analysis. It typically signals that an uptrend is coming to an end and a downtrend may begin. The pattern consists of three peaks:

1. **Left Shoulder**: Price rises and then falls.

2. **Head**: Price rises again, forming a higher peak than the left shoulder, then falls back.

3. **Right Shoulder**: Price rises for a third time, but forms a lower peak similar to the left shoulder.

The **neckline** is drawn across the lows between the two shoulders and the head. The pattern is confirmed when the price breaks below the neckline, often indicating a strong shift from buying to selling pressure.

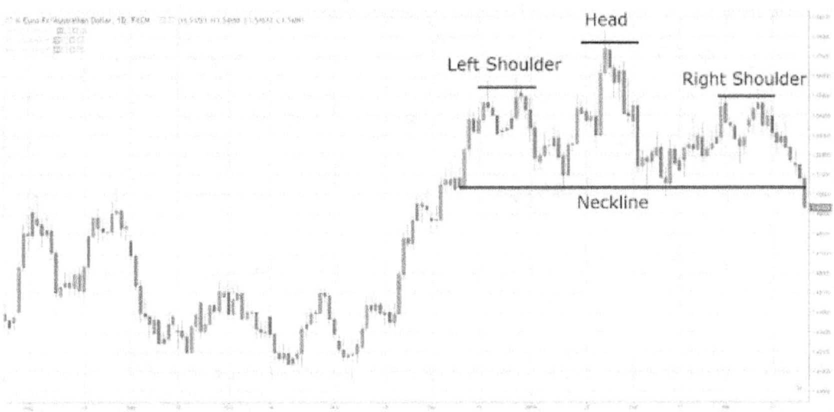

Market Psychology

Uptrend: Buyers control the market initially.

Left Shoulder: First sign of resistance.

Head: Buyers push to a new high, but sellers return.

Right Shoulder: Buyers are weaker, unable to reach previous highs.

Neckline Break: Sellers take full control and a downtrend begins.

The **breakdown** below the neckline is considered the entry point for selling.

Higher volume on the **breakout increases** reliability.

The **target price** is usually estimated by measuring the distance from the head to the neckline and **projecting** it **downward**.

1. REVERSE HEAD AND SHOULDER PATTERN

The **Reverse Head and Shoulders**, also called Inverse Head and Shoulders, is a widely used **bullish reversal chart pattern**. It usually forms after a downtrend and indicates that selling pressure is weakening and buyers may take control.

1. **Left Shoulder**: Price falls and then rises.

2. **Head**: Price falls again to a lower low, then rises back.

3. **Right Shoulder**: Price falls a third time but forms a higher low, similar to the left shoulder.

A **neckline** is drawn across the peaks between the shoulders and the head. The pattern is confirmed when the price **breaks above** the **neckline**, signaling a **potential** trend shift from **bearish to bullish**.

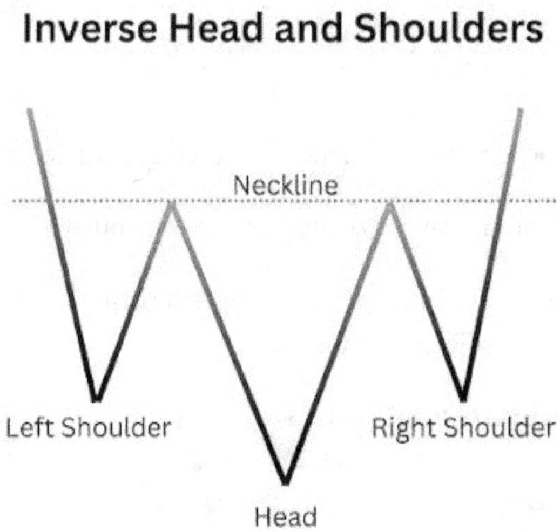

MARKET PSYCHOLOGY:

Downtrend: Sellers dominate at first.

Left Shoulder: First sign of support

Head: Strong selling attempt but buyers return.

Right Shoulder: Sellers weaker; cannot make a new low.

Breakout: Buyers gain strength and may start an uptrend.

A **breakout** above the **neckline** is often used as a **buy** entry.

High trading volume on breakout increases reliability.

The target price is estimated by measuring the distance from the head to the neckline and projecting it upward.

CONTINUATION PATTERNS

1. BULLISH RECTANGLE

A **Bullish Rectangle** is a continuation chart pattern that appears during an existing uptrend. It forms when the price moves sideways between two **horizontal levels**, a resistance at the top and a support at the bottom creating a rectangular shape. This pattern shows a temporary pause in the trend as buyers and sellers battle for control.

During this phase, price repeatedly **bounces** between **support and resistance**, indicating consolidation rather than reversal. The pattern is considered complete when the price breaks above the resistance level, signaling that buyers have regained strength and the uptrend is likely to continue.

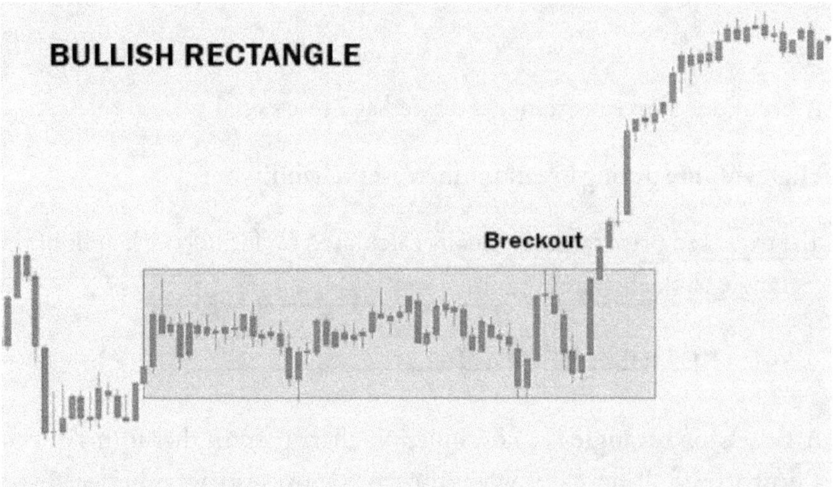

MARKET PSYCHOLOGY

The market is already in an **uptrend**

Buyers push price up to resistance, then sellers push it down to support

This up-down movement continues, forming a rectangle

Once buyers break through resistance, bullish momentum resumes

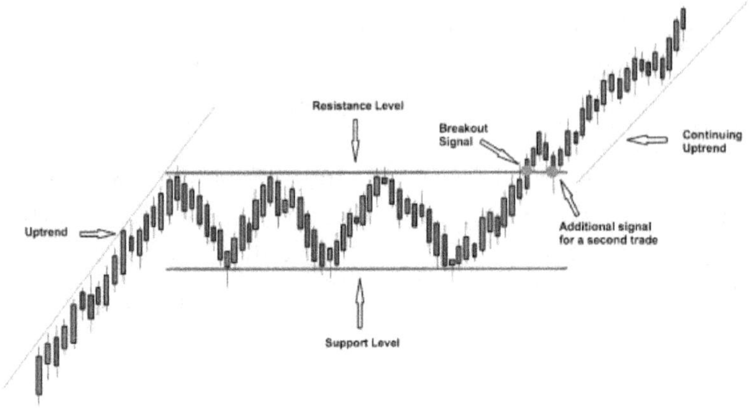

A **breakout** above resistance is treated as a buy signal

High **volume** during **breakout** increases reliability

The expected price target is usually calculated by adding the height of the rectangle to the breakout point

1. BEARISH RECTANGLE

A **Bearish Rectangle** is a continuation chart pattern that forms during a **downtrend**. It develops when the price moves sideways between two horizontal levels, a support at the bottom and a resistance at the top creating a rectangular shape. This pattern shows **temporary consolidation**, where neither buyers nor sellers gain control for a short period.

Price repeatedly moves up and down within these levels, but does not break out either way. The pattern is considered complete when the price breaks below the support level, signaling that sellers have regained dominance and the downtrend is likely to continue.

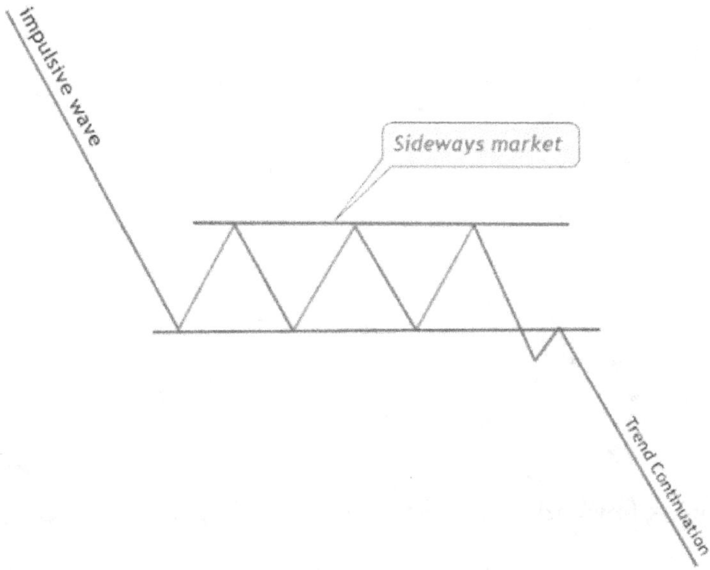

Market Psychology:

The market is already in a **downtrend**

Sellers push price down to support, buyers push it up to resistance

This sideways movement forms a **rectangle consolidation**

When **support breaks**, selling pressure increases and the price **continues falling**

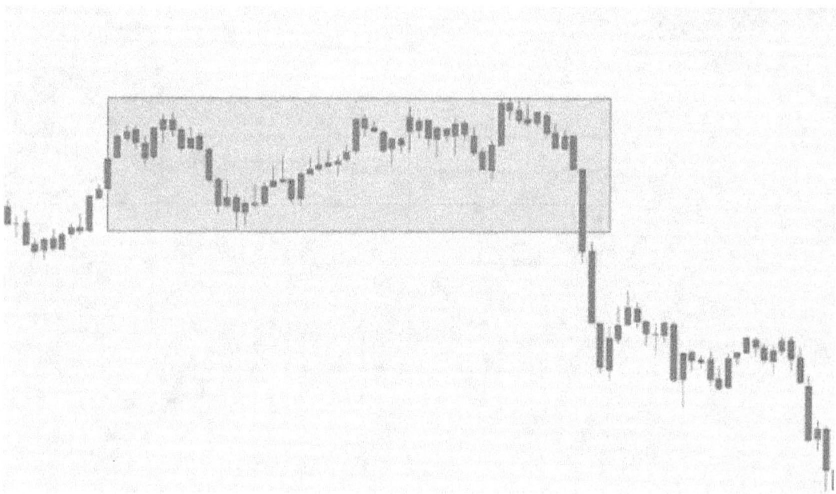

A **breakdown** below support is used as a sell signal

High volume during **breakdown** makes the pattern more reliable

The price target is estimated by **subtracting the height of the rectangle** from the breakdown point

---

NEUTRAL PATTERNS

1. SYMMETRICAL CONTRACTING TRIANGLE PATTERN

A **Symmetrical Contracting Triangle** is a chart pattern that forms when the price begins to **move within a narrowing range**, creating a series of lower highs and higher lows. The trendlines drawn across these highs and lows converge, forming a triangle shape. This pattern represents a period of indecision and consolidation where neither buyers nor sellers are in full control.

This pattern is considered **neutral**, meaning the breakout can occur in either direction , **upward or downward.** However, it usually appears during an **existing trend** and often acts as a **continuation pattern**, meaning the price generally breaks out in the direction of the prior trend.

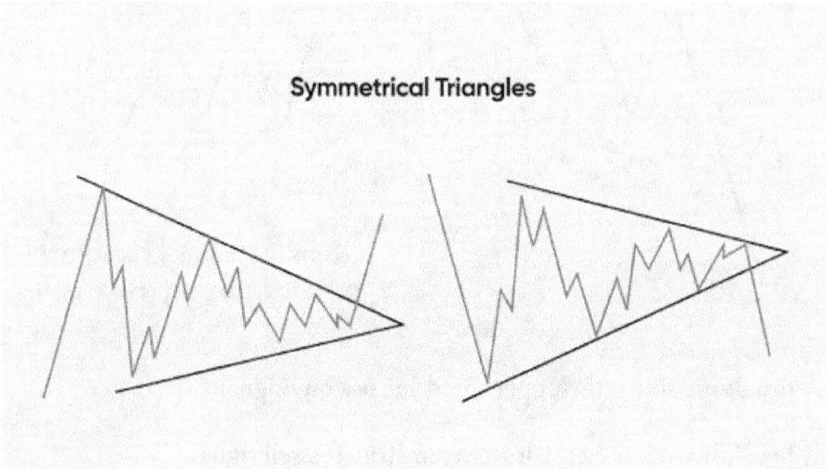

Market Psychology

Price volatility decreases as buyers and sellers become evenly matched

Each rally is weaker and each decline is smaller, forming a tightening structure

Traders wait for a clear breakout before taking positions

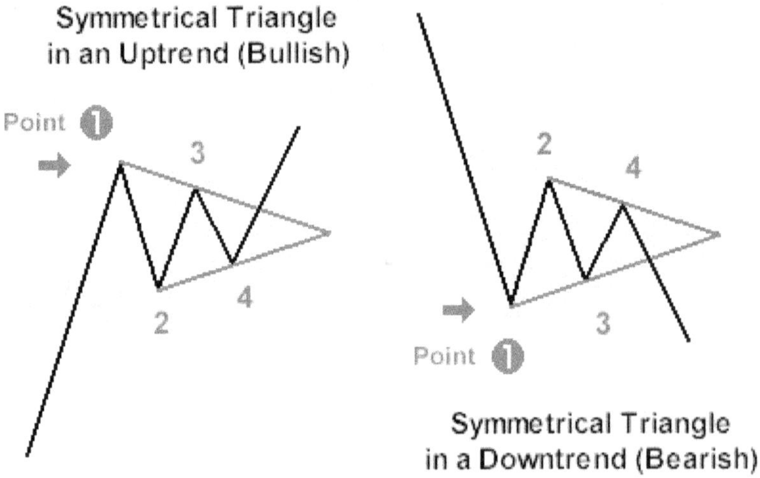

A **breakout** above the upper trendline is a buy signal

A **breakdown** below the lower **trendline** is a sell signal

Breakout volume is important for confirmation

Price targets are often measured by the height of the wide end of the triangle

1. SYMMETRICAL EXPANDING TRIANGLE PATTERN

A **Symmetrical Expanding Triangle** is a chart pattern where the price forms higher highs and lower lows, creating a widening shape. The trendlines drawn along these highs and lows **diverge**, forming a **triangle that expands over time**. This pattern shows increasing market volatility and uncertainty, as both buyers and sellers are aggressively trying to control price direction.

This pattern suggests **instability rather than consolidation**. Unlike contracting triangles, where price becomes quieter, an expanding triangle shows that price swings are getting **larger with time**. It can lead to a breakout in either direction, but the movement afterward is often **strong and rapid** due to the energy built during the expansion phase.

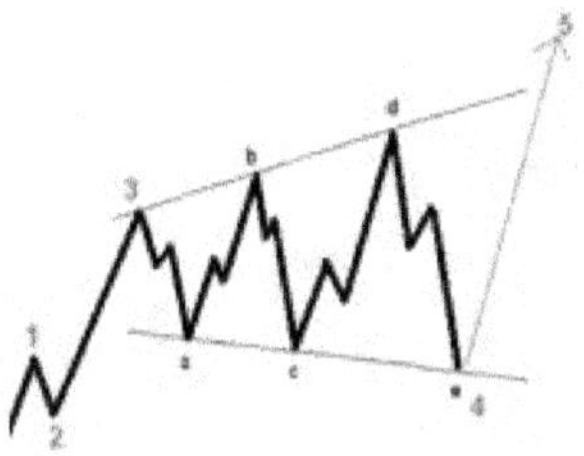

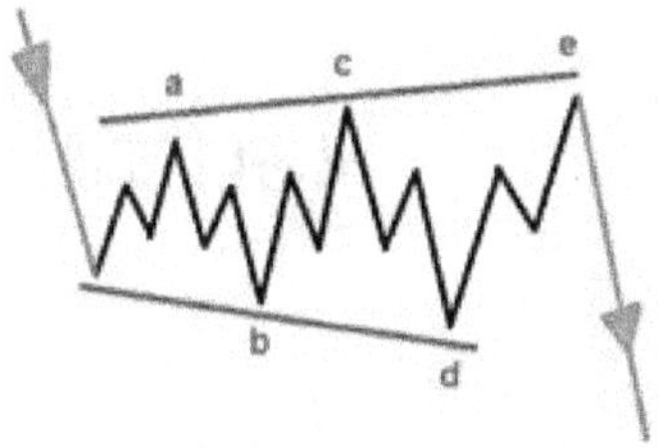

Market Psychology

Higher highs: Buyers are pushing prices further up each time

Lower lows: Sellers are pushing prices further down each time

Market sentiment keeps swinging back and forth

Traders wait for a decisive breakout or breakdown, which often leads to a sharp trend

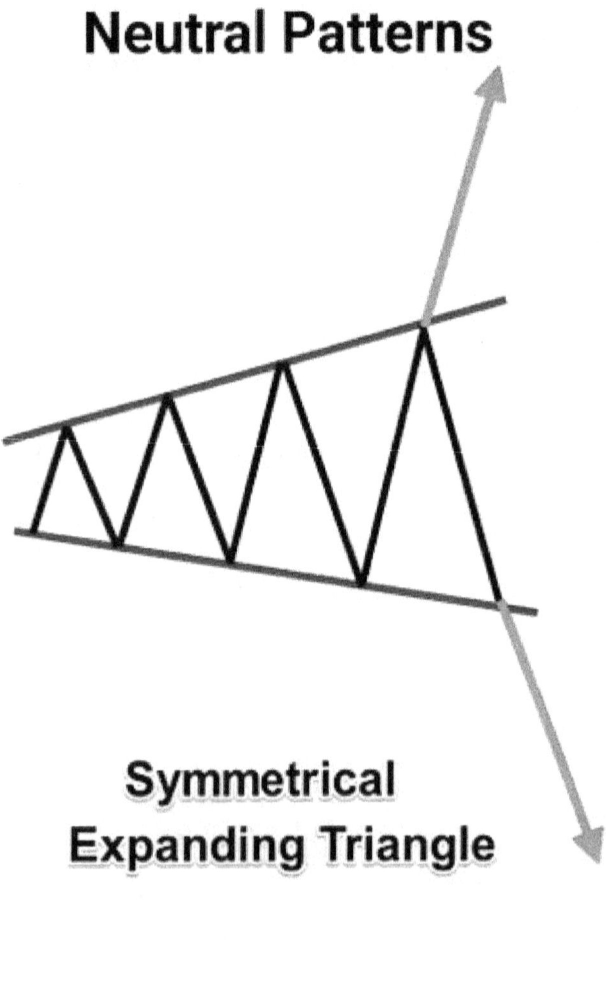
Neutral Patterns
Symmetrical
Expanding Triangle

A **breakout** above the upper trendline signals bullish continuation

A **breakdown below** the lower trendline signals bearish continuation

Volume confirmation is important because **false breakouts are common** in this pattern

Price target is often projected by measuring the widest part of the triangle

---

TO BE CONTINUED.....

www.ingramcontent.com/pod-product-compliance
Lightning Source LLC
LaVergne TN
LVHW022029200926
848481LV00007B/2599
* 9 7 9 8 2 3 1 6 8 3 6 4 2 *